WELCOME TO SONNETVILLE, NEW JERSEY

WELCOME TO SONNETVILLE, NEW JERSEY

POEMS BY

CRAIG MORGAN TEICHER

AMERICAN POETS CONTINUUM SERIES, NO. 184

BOA EDITIONS, LTD. ◎ ROCHESTER, NY ◎ 2021

First Edition
21 22 23 24 7 6 5 4 3 2 1

For information about permission to reuse any material from this book, please contact
The Permissions Company at www.permissionscompany.com or e-mail permdude@
gmail.com.

Publications by BOA Editions, Ltd.—a not-for-profit corporation under NATIONAL
section 501 (c) (3) of the United States Internal Revenue Code—are made ENDOWMENT
possible with funds from a variety of sources, including public funds from $\frac{2}{5}$ ARTS
the Literature Program of the National Endowment for the Arts; the New ═════ arts.gov
York State Council on the Arts, a state agency; and the County of Monroe,
NY. Private funding sources include the Max and Marian Farash Charitable   State of the Arts
Foundation; the Mary S. Mulligan Charitable Trust; the Rochester Area
Community Foundation; the Ames-Amzalak Memorial Trust in memory
of Henry Ames, Semon Amzalak, and Dan Amzalak; the LGBT Fund of   NYSCA
Greater Rochester; and contributions from many individuals nationwide. See Colo-
phon on page 106 for special individual acknowledgments.

Cover Design: Sandy Knight
Interior Design and Composition: Richard Foerster
BOA Logo: Mirko

BOA Editions books are available electronically through BookShare, an online distributor
offering Large-Print, Braille, Multimedia Audio Book, and Dyslexic formats, as well as
through e-readers that feature text to speech capabilities.

Library of Congress Cataloging-in-Publication Data

Names: Teicher, Craig Morgan, 1979– author.
Title: Welcome to Sonnetville, New Jersey : poems / by Craig Morgan Teicher.
Description: First Edition. | Rochester, NY : BOA Editions, Ltd., 2021. | Series: American poets
    continuum series ; no. 184 | Summary: "Neo-confessional poems about moving back to the
    suburbs, raising a family, sustaining a marriage, and facing the humility that comes with not
    being young anymore"— Provided by publisher.
Identifiers: LCCN 2020044420 (print) | LCCN 2020044421 (ebook) | ISBN
    9781950774258 (paperback) | ISBN 9781950774265 (ebook)
Subjects: LCGFT: Poetry.
Classification: LCC PS3620.E4359 W45 2021 (print) | LCC PS3620.E4359 (ebook) |
    DDC 811/.6—dc23
LC record available at https://lccn.loc.gov/2020044420
LC ebook record available at https://lccn.loc.gov/2020044421

BOA Editions, Ltd.
250 North Goodman Street, Suite 306
Rochester, NY 14607
www.boaeditions.org
A. Poulin, Jr., Founder (1938–1996)

This book is for Brenda, with whom . . .

CONTENTS

Still, there was always the feeling that one would get around to being young again. And that when one was young again, life would resume the course from which it had so shockingly deviated.

—Deborah Eisenberg

I still wallow like Phil

—The Microphones, "Great Ghosts"

PEERS

I'm thinking of you beautiful
and young, of me young

and confused and maybe
beautiful. There were lots of us—

these were our twenties, when,
post-9/11, we were about to

inherit the world, and we had no idea
what to do with it. And look

what we did, and we didn't.
And now look at us, and it.

We turned away for a blip, started
whispering, kissing, had kids,

bought houses, changed bulbs,
submitted claims, changed channels,

FaceTimed, streamed, upgraded,
were two-day-shipped to, and midway

through our prime earning years
we look up again, decades groggy,

decades late. *Forgive us*, we thought—
but now it doesn't matter. These are our

outcomes, consequences, faults,
forties, when the hourglass

is beeping and bleak and people
like us have memories like this

and wonder if the beauty that's left
is really still beautiful, if it was.

I AM A FATHER NOW

I am a father now, an unprecedented thing
I never was before and have always been,
preparing, preparing since I was born a father's son,
and not a mother's daughter. Plus I married a daughter's
mother, little did I know. But how could I?
It had only been a moment since I arrived—
I was barely conceived on one of time's
unremembered nights, and suddenly I woke
with a child crying in each ear, these years
like the coils of a patient snake that has lovingly
nibbled and swallowed me countlessly.
I am diminished to a great height, the ceiling
of the world tickling the tips of my lost hairs.
I loom like the moon over two baby baboons,
my helpless, hopeful hobbits, one for each
leaden eye. I might be just like my father's
father for all I know. I could be the bearer
of my mother's father's nose, and look
what I've done with it, seat of my driving glasses.
I'm the lover, quietly, furtively, of the bearer
of my daughter and son—the fever of our sex
shakes the house we uphold, but let's not wake
the children here or next door or next door to that.
Or let's wake them up and play with them now
while no one's looking, for joy is always
our secret, the secret of this hurried, harried life
without horses. I sleep when I can, and I can't die.
I have never been as mortal as now. I bend low,
my back aching and breaking under grateful weight.
No matter—I'll grow another. I have my children
to thank for my bending body, which is born
a hundred times each day, dying every breath.

ASSURANCES 1

When the time comes, it will be the first time.

~

A life, even a long one, is really very short. Even the littlest book, a page, a paragraph, a word, takes many lives to write.

~

Almost there . . . and then? I start again, but not, of course, from the beginning.

~

Word problem: I am now as old as my parents were when they were my parents. My children are as old as I was. How many apples does Jenny have left?

~

How many times each day do I ask myself whether I have accomplished what I had hoped. "You haven't failed," I tell myself. But how much better it would be to reset everything today, to name a new goal for the next forty years, and to be forty again forty years from now.

~

"At five, your whole life is imaginary," said my eight-year-old daughter. At forty, I say, only half your life is imaginary. But which half?

~

You know it's bad for you, but you do it anyway, because it isn't bad for you *yet*.

~

Has it chosen me already, the disease that will kill me?

~

Happy birthday, Craig. Happy day after your birthday, Craig. And so on.

~

If I had it all to do over again, I would pause for a moment first. Anticipation? Hesitation?

((1))

WELCOME TO SONNETVILLE, NEW JERSEY

SON

I don't even know where my father lives.
I know his number, and whenever
I call he answers and gives
the usual update about getting together
with the stepkids and their kids,
about the latest minor crises
with his health, about what he did
with Maryanne for their anniversary.
His house is somewhere in Connecticut
near where he lived before.
It's been easy not to go there, but
I know I should—there won't always be more
time. There will always be less.
I don't even know my father's address.

DISTILLATION

Well, first you were born.
Childhood stretched toward forever.
Then, suddenly, your life was torn
into before and after.

Before, you felt everything:
green leaves quivering,
the soft dance of dust
through rays of sun. You must

have somehow forgotten.
After, years passed almost instantly—
When did all of it happen?

Didn't you just turn ten, or forty?
When was your daughter born?
How is it now already?

DROP OFF

Simone's kindergarten is at the top of our street.
This morning, holding hands, we eagerly trudge
uphill. She waits in her class line while I meet
the other parents. My work won't wait, but I've no grudge
against these fifteen sociable minutes. After checking phones,
we introduce ourselves, wearing our kids like name tags—
Hello I'm Alice's; Hello I'm Simone's—
reborn as the ones who packed their lunch bags,
hurried them—*socks, now! Shoes!*—into neon clothes,
stuffed pancakes and yogurt into their mouths,
and brought them to this sea-edge, where, in droves,
they embark upon the slow journey toward themselves.
It's just like my old school—here I am across that sea,
back where I started—but I'm my mom; Simone is me.

TYING A GARBAGE BAG

Looking down at my hands, I see myself
as if for the first time for the thousandth time
drawing into a bow the awkward leaves
of the black trash bag into which I have just deftly
dumped a plastic wastebasket full of tissues and
tampon wrappers, plus a flower pot brimming
with cigarette butts. I find myself admiring the swift
dexterity with which I fashion, almost effortlessly,
the weird knot to seal off the bag from the world
its contents had been contaminating. So now
it takes only this to dazzle my pride.
I had dreamed of splitting the wind
with my lips, but will settle, for now, for being
the unacknowledged legislator of this bag.

MARRIAGE ABSTRACT

Arguments taint our mouths like spice.
Opening and closing doors, we rhyme.
The house creaks to pass, or mark, the time
under our bare feet, the mortgage like ice
we skate above the bottomless water.
It mustn't crack; we can't afford to fall.
I love you like my hands, which haul
the money in. Into our laps spill daughter
and son. We are drowning in wine and beer,
carrying each other across these rooms,
glasses filled above our brims. We consume
ourselves in our big shared bed. Here,
plans overrun our mouths, all synonyms.
You used to be her. I used to be him.

EARLY TO BED

You conk out as soon as the children are down,
softly snoring while I putter around.
Other nights it's me asleep first—
whoever is more soul-tired, whoever feels worse.
On your late nights, you're up till two or three,
and when you come in, you vaguely wake me
fussing with the bathroom door or your phone.
We share a bed but fall asleep alone.
On my late nights, I write, work on a review,
savor my privacy, miss you.
I binge on Netflix and sneak into bed.
You roll over, protecting your head.
We try to talk during crowded weekend days.
Simone interrupts what each of us says.

LIFTED

Well, I guess no one can have everything.
I must learn to celebrate when I fail.
Inner growth and fortitude follow the sting,
right? Won't I rise with holy wind in my sails?
Yet *they* always seem to get what *I* want,
door after door flung open. Why are
the keepers of doors, who haunt
the hopeful halls of fate and desire
so partial to them, but not to me?
Yes, I *do* feel sorry for myself—don't, brother,
pretend the bitter blanket of self-pity
hasn't warmed your bones. It's not lovers
or fame I crave, nor even happiness, particularly.
Only to be lifted, just once, above all others.

((2))

A DREAM

ASSURANCES 2

I am, basically, a good person—I know this because not even once have I locked my children in the house alone, gotten in my car, and driven forever.

~

But I am an artist, I say, as I dump another load of cans into the recycling bin.

~

Fear knows the story isn't *about* anything.

~

I take out the garbage every Sunday and Wednesday night. And yet, there is always more garbage. So far, there have always been more nights.

~

I wish I could listen to music all day . . . I suppose I can, but that's not what I'm wishing for.

~

I can't help but feel that raindrops are targeting me, that puddles shift underfoot to soak my pant cuffs, that my luck is specifically mine.

~

Thirsty, I am lucky enough to have a solvable problem.

~

No grain is too tiny to grind.

A DREAM I NEVER HAD

in which a van
pulls up the dark driveway,
its long lights parting

the heavy night. The side
door slides open and there
is my mother, beckoning.

"Quick," she says, "get in
before your father finds out
I'm not dead anymore."

"Don't you want to meet
your grandkids?" I ask.
"There isn't time for that,

and you won't miss them
where we're going."
"Where are we going?"

"Back, obviously, to
redo everything better.
I want to be happy this time,"

she says. "What will I do?"
I ask. "I'm too old
to be your son." "We'll see,"

she says, "but we have to go
now." "Come on, Marcia,"
I hear someone hiss

from the driver's seat.
"Come on," says my mom.
"Daddy"—I hear Simone calling

from just inside the house.
"I have to check, Mom. Wait—
please," I say, but already

the van is backing out,
the lights recoiling.
Already I am awake.

GUSH

The geese are flying back—that seems
                                a decent place to start.
They're honking their damn horns across
the wide night sky.
                        Why not? The neighbors'
car honks too, another omen.
They seem to want to check on the lock
                                    on their car.
You imagine them fumbling for the fob from bed,
just in case.
                    The trash is out. Distant windows glow
yellow, flicker blue. All of this is addressed
to you.

~

You have no enemies, not real ones.
                            There are places you could go
for danger, where you're unwanted, where,
even from a distance, your cheek and your hair
mean something, but you won't
                                go there.
Your fears eddy around the house—
                                your son's fitful sleep,
the daughter you must pass everything to.
And you know, already, no one has a clue
                        what you're talking about.
This megaphone—who gave it you?—echoes
a couple of blocks at most
                        before your voice gets lost.

~

First word, best word. Second word, worst.
No. And never mind. Nevertheless,
there's a pinprick in your chest:
                                all the light is gushing out.
This street would be so dark otherwise.
                                I think you might
be the source of all that
                    window light, of all those geese.
Think of the consequences—
only you can handle
                your candle.
Only you can slump
                    on your life's one rump.

⁓

Fold your cold
            hands in your lap. Act like
a patient etherized upon a table.
                    You must do all that you're able.
Your needle swings from empty to full.
                    Cotton, Pyrex, velvet, wool.
So you see, this is just another cold night.
                    The lamp sighs artificial light.
        But there's nothing so bad about that.
Born again, be a cat,
allergic to yourself, quiet as a spike.

⁓

There's no escape, or if there is
                    this is it. Can you crawl
through a pinprick? Do you know how
to honk? When you close your eyes, the lights
don't go out,
            they go in. The end is near.
            [Add great last line here.]

POLISHING THE MAMMALS

There were four—an elk,
a house cat, a porpoise, and
an anxious naked mole rat. All
were dirty and in need of brightening.
I brought out the old rag box
and got right down to it.

Work on the elk went quickly.
Despite his size and ragged coat,
not to mention the latticework of
horns branching above me like
the canopy of the primordial forest,
his contours were as I expected.

He was cooperative, seemingly
eager to get gussied up. I did all
I could and sent him on his way.
The cat was reluctant to submit:
she felt I intended to do
for her what she was perfectly

capable of handling herself.
Nonetheless, she was accustomed
to human ministrations, so
finally settled into my lap
as if doing me a favor. I was able
to get her gleaming like a new spoon

in under an hour. You might think
a porpoise, always submerged,
would not need polishing, but
it was as if she'd spent her life
in a foul oil bath rather than the sea.
I spent all of Wednesday and much

of Thursday on her. When she
finally slipped through my fingers
that afternoon, splashing
like a clever idea back into the surf,
though she was somewhat better,
she still looked mostly mucky.

I think I will always be covered
in guilt when I think of her,
so like me in many ways, yet so
alien. It's the naked mole rat,
however, that's giving me the most
trouble. Smallish and pink, a satisfying

tube of flesh, a shivering penis
or the inside of an old lover's arm,
it feels both wrong and right.
I can't discern a gender, yet
I find myself unable to resist worrying
its soft skin with my fingers, like

some smooth and comforting
stone, like my baby blanket. And it
was already so worried when I took
it out of the packaging. It hates,
I believe, to be away from its
colony of dozens of siblings

and cousins, but I'm just not done
with my work. I'm not sure I've even
managed to begin. But I can't
put it down—I won't! We all have
our vices—I seem to have discovered
a new one of mine. I think I thought

—or I hoped, at least—I'd found
a job that truly suited me,

a role, however unnecessary,
for which I was designed by
the great unbelieved-in administrator
in the sky. But, alas, I find

my energies once again
diverted into a secondary, or tertiary,
channel, another eddying place.
Soon I'll rub right through this rat
and want another. I'm making no
progress toward curing myself

of my inner urges. Do you think
I intended to go on this long?
Do you honestly believe this
is how I'd hoped to spend
your attention, now that I finally
have it? There is some holy

and wondrous thing pent up in me,
I know, waiting and wishing
for the light, but scrub as I will,
it remains buried beneath grime and
perversities. I am a born shipwright
raised in a landlocked city, lost

and calling to you, my friends,
for far longer than my little life,
for forever, sounding my dull horn
from the foggy depths of my eyes,
the good dream of your answers
carrying me nowhere like a breeze.

THE CHORUS

1

It's, you know, the part that repeats,
the bit you're supposed
to remember, the bit that bears

repeating, the part that means
something new
each time, something different,

and the same thing, too,
the thing you can't forget,
that gets stuck in your head.

So, like, *childhood*
is endless and over
almost as soon as it begins?

Yeah, like that. Ten years
shrinks like the pages
of a water-damaged book.

No, the pages don't really shrink
or shrivel, they crinkle, get kinda
crisp and brittle, but

time's like that, a wrinkle,
and suddenly you've been
married as long as

you were ever a kid,
ever awash in the interminable
Thursday of your first ten years, when

three months was an eon, when,
like, *childhood was endless*
and over as soon as it began.

See what I did there? Shifted
the refrain into the middle.
Yeah, time is like that, and

2

suddenly your newborn
is ten and your wife
is celebrating the birthday

only grown-ups do,
and you must be older
than your mom was

at your age, and it's not
Thursday—was it ever? And the two
pills you have to take every night.

How is it Sunday, I mean
Monday, this morning, your alarm,
your coffee grumbling, thunder,

and the kids (two of them,
suddenly) are out the door, and
their childhood is

endless and already over
as soon as it begins, and
you're on the bus to work. See what

I did there? I don't. The four
pills you have to take three
times every day, you might

3

as well already be
at your desk, your deathbed,
holding your daughter's

grown-up hand, you
hope, the hospital calm and
clean like the one your mother

died in, and there's hopefully
money somewhere to take care
of everything, and this

is like *childhood, endless
and over as soon as it begins*,
or as close as you'll ever get

again—see what I did
there? Did you
see? Did anyone?

ODE

How new
            everything is
to the puppy. Invited

by everything, she only
moves *toward*.

Strangers clap and bend
to embrace her.
            I find myself
recoiling more and more
from more.

No one would blame me.
No one would notice.
            The puppy: all

eyes,
      all open, and here I am
like a painter lost
to obscurity, living his gone
years in his mother's basement
until she dies and he moves upstairs.

But the puppy can live forever
                        gladly panting
in love's cupped hands.
She can drink deeply
from puddles.
She fears only
            what she cannot understand—
large trash cans, roaring
motorcycles, the distant dark
into which she cranes her neck,

immovable
        before the night's last walk.

Aren't you alike in so many ways?

You would clutch her
           to your heart,
force her in there.
She squirms in your arms like freedom.

THE TRUE WORK

The worm will always worm
its way under a rock, some bark,
                            some wet old wood.
Startled by light, exhausted
by company, the worm would rather munch
                            a bunch
of dirt. It's not waiting for the end of the world.
It's never heard of the world.

~

I've heard of it.
It's where the worm lives.
It also has
                many other
distinguishing features.
I won't tax your patience
by listing them here.
                Maybe just a few . . .
Sunsets, pacific garbage patch, alpacas.
                        You'll know it when you see it.

~

The fox will always outfox
the hare.
        The turtle will never tattle.
Slow and steady, he'll win
                the race
through the sheer force
                    of his integrity.
You'll look up to him down there.
He's a hero in a half shell.

I've got a camera trained on the pore
                    out of which
the light is scheduled to ooze.
You bring popcorn
                    and a six pack.
I'm having a listening party.
Visit poreparty.com.
Please.
They're monitoring
                    my traffic.
You can write off your attention
as an in-kind donation.

The mood saunters in, tossing
his jacket on the couch.
He's a bad mood
so the jacket is leather.
He's cool without trying.
In fact, that's why he's cool.
We dropped two notches
and got taken down a peg
when he arrived,
sweeping across the verse
of tonight like a sweet solo.
We all looked down at our shitty shoes.
He's so funny we're afraid
to laugh.

Company exhausts me.
Like poetry.
Like a balloon who forgot his air.

Like when you get a haircut
         and everyone says "nice hair,"
which means it looked like crap before,
which is why you linger
beer can in hand
         by the door.

The work is always the work.
               It's hard.
You've got to stand on your own two feet
because you gave up your chair.
         You were being courteous,
hoping your mom would smile
         from the beyond.
That's the way she raised you.
Nobody promised the party
        would be fun.

DRAWING

I'm bad at it, capable only
of lazy shapes to which I add eyes
and a mouth to make little monsters.

A vague happiness grows as they appear
under my uncertain, imprecise hand,
slightly creepy, sometimes

cute, and accurate in a way
writing never is. I feel no
temptation to show my sketches

to anyone, even Brenda, my love,
whom I always wish will be proud
and impressed. Sometimes, lately,

when I think of her saying something
she might say to or about
our kids, I swap, for an instant,

my mother's face for Brenda's, but it's
Brenda's voice ringing clear from her mouth.
What might that mean? It's sort of

comforting, and also weird. Brenda
is now the same age my mother was
when she died. Oh! Forty-eight—

half a life and then some, all
she had, my childhood still
unfurling—I held on to it as if trying

to pin a simmering wave to the shore.
I might still be trying. But what's that
got to do with Brenda? What just

happened? Suddenly, I find myself
beached, lost whale gasping
out of its world on that thought.

DIALOGUE BETWEEN MARRIED POETS

Why must you write so much? Do you have to?
Every night? We have a couple hours awake
after the kids go to bed, and I miss you.

All these anxious poems are my safe way through
the night, during which, otherwise, I'd shake.
I'd be no good to you, I'm afraid. I'm afraid I have to.

You don't think I'm anxious, shaking, spent, too?
Our children demand almost all my mind; what's left is baked.
Forget my past. I miss *my* mind, too, but choose you.

But why don't *you write—you have the same few*
hours as me. Didn't we make
this promise—to enable each other to do what we have to?

Of course we did, but you see how you skew
my words. I'll write when I can, but you take
too much from the shared pot. I'll miss you,

you'll miss me, saying love was a train that flew
past. Did either of us get on? But stake
out your writing nights—you insist you have to.
I'll adjust; I always do. But you'll miss me missing you.

DREAD ON THE EVE OF MY DAUGHTER'S SEVENTH BIRTHDAY PARTY

Soon, thirty children will descend
on our house, hungry
for cupcakes and friends
and games. We have filled three

piñatas with candy and toys
and pushed couches and tables
aside to make room for boys
and girls wherever we're able.

At the center of our home
a sinkhole gapes wide.
I thought I was born to be alone,
to silently, patiently hide

inside shrubs, behind doors,
or amidst coats, like a bomb
in the sale racks of clothing stores
while, anxiously, my mom

shopped. Have I been
waiting till tomorrow to blow?
What, when I am Simon,
will I say? *Simon says go*

away. Simon says, hey,
the party is over. Have some
cake. Aha! Simon didn't say—
You're out! Go home!

But, no, tomorrow's the result
of my lifetime's worth of choices.
And yes, it *will* be my fault
if my daughter's friends' voices

aren't gleeful. I owe her happiness
if only because it was I, not she,
who asked for all of this:
marriage, house, for her to be.

If I'd really wanted solitude,
an old bench by a calm lake,
a quiet dog with whom to brood
over endless days and make

sad poems about loneliness
and artful despondency,
a hermit's wise and barren bliss,
I'd have chosen differently.

THE SOLUTION

Throw money at it. Pray.
Meditate for ten minutes two times every day.
When in doubt, delay.

Get to bed tonight by ten.
Don't try that bullshit again.
Rejoin the gym. Go. But when?

Try to look at it differently.
Forget about me.
Skip therapy.

Stay awake till your work is done
and your heart weighs only half a ton.
Drink like it's fun.

It's too cold. Stay inside.
Your mother lived until she died.
Spit out mouthfuls of pride.

Just let it go.
It's beautiful, all that snow.
She's right, you know.

Wipe the crap off your boots.
Too much sweetness dilutes.
Pull it up by the roots,

don't just snip the stem.
Listen, or don't listen, to them.
Ignore the problem.

((3))

AMBIVALENCE AND OTHER CONUNDRUMS

REGRET

Beckoned by the things you'd go back for but can't, you push on, dragging the past behind like a vestigial tail, lizardo, can-kicker, backward-glancer tripping over a ripple in the road.

Yet you do go on, determined to get to where your dreams can expand to fill the space of their container, the wild sky just beyond your mind. It's a shame to be cynical here, in only paragraph two, but necessary for the sake of the truth, which, dressed as the obvious, is counting on you.

You *can* go back. But only after you have read this far—the beginning only matters from a certain distance.

Two pigeons meet in the park and fight over a bit of bread and have no bearing on any of this. You can follow them into the night: they coo like little fuck machines outside some apartment window, but instead your mother is dead and you are too busy digging a tunnel back to childhood with a spoon.

WHAT YOU LOVE

Well, you've got to do something. On the one hand, the options are limitless. On the other, obviously, most options are unavailable to you. Those that are are obscured by the black wallowing of possibility.

How many times did you tell yourself you knew what you wanted?

Some people are able to follow a single desire like a rope tied off just beyond the horizon. Some, annoyingly, will even say it's a curse; of course it isn't. How justified is our hatred of the blessèd and their blessings.

It's good to have a hobby. I read books about jazz while listening to albums in the evening, after work, once the kids are in bed. My wife thinks it's noise but puts up with it, barely. I can't decide whether to go on or off my diet: indulge or withhold, sew happiness while I can or fortify my character . . . a hobby offers at least the illusion of a still point toward which one's compass needle is trained.

A calling in life is just another decision, meaningless in the grand scheme, of which there isn't one; no one is calling. The one who feels called is pushing against the great, indifferent weight which falls like an ocean on everyone's shoulders—thankfully we are all in this together, Atlas and friends.

You must follow your heart, though all hearts are heading to the same place, a place for hearts only.

It takes 10,000 hours of repetition to achieve mastery, but don't think about that or you'll never start; blades of grass, mounds of earth, hills and mountains all rise into the one sky.

DIGGITY DOG

Oh boy does he like digging! Oh boy oh boy he loves it! What's he digging for? Nothing! He just loves getting the dirt out of the way to get to more dirt! If he finds anything, who cares?

A coin, an old wooden widget, a gold tooth, the missing key to the missing lock to the missing door to the heart inside the heart's heart? Whatever! It's all more dirt to him—just get it out of the way to dig up more dirt. And at the bottom? What about when he gets to the bottom?

Well, even he knows there's no bottom, nothing there, it's nowhere, just more and deeper and more, just keep digging. It just gets a little bit harder, it's harder and harder and harder, but oh boy digging is great!

LIST

He is a maker of lists, things to do, things desired, things wrong. He checks things off, crosses them out, starts a new sheet of paper, starts again. He loves that feeling, the sensation of the pen not erasing but effacing what had previously been an order, defacing it.

He likes calendars, lists of days, boxes unchecked, soon to be crossed off. Time stretches out before him, something to get done, something to be done with.

He wakes up each morning, pees, brushes his teeth—well, some mornings he doesn't brush, hasn't yet had time to list brushing as a task—and pulls on fresh underwear, pants, a shirt. Then he has his coffee, his cereal, his toast. Then he must get out the door, go to the bus, travel to work.

Once there, he makes his first list, partitions his day into what must be accomplished by the end, and begins working. E-mail Rhonda, check over the report, affix his signature. Get cash, meet Arnold for lunch, pay the bill, save the receipt. Get through the afternoon, check Facebook, shut down the computer, go home.

He watches TV, plays some music, eats some food. He reads his book, puts it away, picks it up again. Now he brushes his teeth, takes off his clothes, gets into bed, shuts off the light.

Days line up neatly like stones on a path, like bridges leading to other bridges, like lily pads lined up to oblivion. He crosses off Monday, Tuesday, Wednesday, Thursday, Friday, birthday, someday.

He is lonely, excited, hopeful, despondent. He knows these feelings pass like lines on a page, like lines on the highway, like lines in his face. This is only his life, any life, every life, ticking away, ticking down. Before sleeping, he thinks of his one wish, his hope, his—he would like to think—destiny: a line running through everything and beyond, a line he can follow even as he is drawing it, something already done that he is still doing, the past ahead of him, the end behind him, his safe terror, the last beginning, the first end, this that, that this, waves succeeding one another, promise and prophesy, his reach and his grasp, I and thou, and so on.

HOMUNCULUS

I need a hug. I need to fuck. I need you to stop editing my every utterance—since when am I so shy?

I know you hate me, that you'd leave if you could, set up shop inside someone with more pluck and verve, but you can't, if only because happy someones never hear their tiny voices, and you'd hate that.

When I can feel your little love, it's like a sun rising inside me over a wide, singing valley. It's my name they're singing over and over—*Craig, Craig, Craig*—and the song is what's raising the sun.

IMMORTALITY

I feel like Emily Dickinson did, running her pale finger over each blade of grass, then caressing each root in the depths of the earth's primeval dirt, each tip tickling heaven's soft underbelly. I feel like Emily alone in her room, her hands folded neatly in her lap, waiting forever for one of those two daguerreotypes to embalm her unprecedented soul.

At my most attuned, the present is a pair of wings stretching forever in all directions, flapping calmly, calmly flapping. But as soon as I notice how happy I am, how close to the sun, there I go plummeting into the background of the same damn painting as ever.

If I could reach my hand out to you now, would you take it? How do you think it would feel? Warm and soft and certain? Or like Emily's: clammy and brittle as hardened paste? Is that not how you imagine her hands? Look again—they were like that, otherwise she could never, would never, have written those poems.

LOVE

He gives and his secret is he expects the beloved to give precisely as much in exchange. He worships in exchange for worship befitting a returning hero whose heroism is worship.

And so the exact price of love is love that is exactly alike, which no love is—one's rose is another's ring. Lover and beloved are always accounting, always paying and collecting the debts, constantly tallying, trading places, now one looming over the other like a colossal tax.

In arrears the lovers need not cleave to one another. Bonded by their debt, they can only move so far, only come so close, before what each owes pulls like a leash.

DRUNKENNESS

Sip by sip, life becomes tolerable, then pleasant, then milky—as soft and gregarious as a lamb. The promises you made seem silly and unimportant, old pieces of paper crumpled at the bottom of your bag. You are asleep before you realize, and there was no cow blocking the path toward your dreams, which carried you all the way to morning, when life intervened, a fact smack in the face.

Now the long day stands before you, with its thousands of gnats horroring every possible path.

You had promised yourself, years and years ago, never to drink alone, like your father drank. Then you thought one or two might be OK. Then, after many drinks, many evenings spent stewing in your sour juices, the sin you'd committed fell so far into the past, an apology wouldn't matter. So now all the evenings roll in this way, moist and comforting, hugging you how you always needed to be hugged.

Maybe age will set in like this too, so slowly you won't have to notice, except for a few acidic moments that will be easy to black out. Hopefully death will be like entering a dream half-awake, half in control, just enough to slip into the swampy drama.

Even those who cry and lament and rage when you die will die too, their echoes far too faint to trace to a source. For now, sleep well. Not even happiness feels this good.

DISAPPOINTMENT

It's where we go to rest from happiness.

WORRY

All the worrier wants is love, like anyone. But he won't seize it for himself; he needs you to come to him, admiring the way he keeps the background safe for all.

He can't—maybe you're right, he *won't*—descend the pole into the heart of the burning house, seek the hotspot between the sheets. But someone fastidious must man the radar, someone, unlike you, who is happy in the lukewarm broth between choices.

One part of him is forever holding his foot above its first step, waiting for the all-clear that can never come. Another part is waiting for you—he may move if you take his hand.

FABLE OF THE BARKING DOGS

A dog barks in the distance. Then another dog barks in answer. Then another, from a different direction. Soon you feel yourself surrounded by dogs barking in answer to one another, a little community spreading the news.

How you would love to be one of them—knowing just what to say and to whom.

In the next life, you find you have been born a dog, and it is as wonderful as you had hoped. You live in a lovely neighborhood, with a loving family to feed you and plenty of trees to piss on and earth to dig holes in. Each night, you join the barking chorus . . .

Oh, if only . . . No, it is still this very same life, this very same night, and the barking dogs are still filling the distance.

FABLE OF THE MAN BY THE WATER

A man stops and stares at the water for a long time, looking for something. A while later, he walks away.

You see him from a distance. You are sitting, watching, you realize, the man watching the water. Did he find what he was looking for? You decide to approach the water to see if you can find it, too, some meaning perhaps, some small vision.

When you come near enough to see the ripples approaching the edge at which you stand, you have your answer, or, really, two possibilities: either he did not find what he was looking for because it was not there, or he did, and he took it away with him.

((4))

Welcome (Back) to Sonnetville, New Jersey

ASSURANCES 3

Compromise: when both sides give up simultaneously.

~

Whose children are we now that we have children?

~

Finally I have all the power I've always craved—I can make choices!
Only, I don't want to. Please, love, choose for me. What do *you*
want to order for dinner?

~

It's highly pressurized—this life, this marriage, this body, this
bottle, this bubble, this self, this cell, this system. If there is no
one to hear it, or if no one cares, does it ever explode? Of course,
but the explosion is just a natural part of this system, this cell, this
self. The bubble bursts, the bottle is opened, the body dies. This
is marriage, life.

~

Parenthood: the tedium of precious moments. The preciousness
of tedious moments. The memories of so many moments, which,
in retrospect, were both unspeakably precious and so numbingly
tedious that one wouldn't wish them on one's enemies. And yet one
would never leave one's children in the care of one's enemies, if
one actually had any actual enemies, rather than people one simply
found too tedious. See how hard I try to escape the tedium, writing
tautologies at night while the children sleep, when all I want is
those precious moments back. No matter how many times I watch
videos of my daughter, she will never be that toddler again. I am

my own enemy, rushing to the next moment, and then through it.
If I woke her now, my daughter would only be confused.

~

War is failed conversation.

~

Sex is conversation consummated, almost, sort of.

SOME SUNDAY

The family sits staring at separate screens.
On this new day, everyone is given

her own eyes, his own sights to see.
The same clock tells each a different time,

each hour so stuffed with slow seconds
that today lasts months, a month

swept under a blink of an eye. What
do I remember? Cal spinning circles

on the living room floor, his poignant,
inarticulate cries filling my mind like a bell.

Simone scattershot launching her bright questions.
Brenda worrying a whirlwind. I'm somewhere

off to one side, egging the hour on. Take
a long look at us, a picture no one is taking.

FOLDED NOTE

It's too cold for the first night
of a new season. All gone,
the neighbors' cars. Are you alone?
Where are they? Perhaps the flight,

the one carrying your daughter and wife,
is delayed? But didn't they go by bus?
Is everything portentous?
Is everything your life?

You're waiting, obviously, for
anything to change: maybe a door
will open, a way through the wall;
maybe a folded note, a surprise call

will pry your heart's elastic pocket.
Or not. *Quick*—try to lock it.

MARRIAGE ABSTRACT

Finally, after a certain amount of time—say,
ten years—or a number of kids—say, two—I
wonder whether the marriage outpaces its love
story. Now is it a partnership? Have the lovers
become administrators of a shared project:
the survival and success of the family, a sly race
against neighbors, against adherents to opposing
beliefs, against the past? Father and mother
may be merely planners, workers, executors; the children
are the product, as is the house, the jobs, all
unfurling like a bright banner proclaiming . . . *what*?
That we are alive, our children thrive in our new
town, and we have not become our parents,
though we look like them and we act like them.

WHO CARES

Mumbling to myself, no one stares.
I lecture to the street, but who cares?

My mother died when I was a child.
All my life is a quest for who cares.

Time runs backwards as I tick off days
searching the old mirror for new cares.

I built the corral I won't pass beyond,
lowing to beckon a keeper who cares.

This poem's going better than I thought
it would, it's true, but do you care?

All my choices have led me right here,
to this chair, to typing *who cares*.

Craig, this is the only life you'll get.
It must be you who cares.

LAKE GEORGE, AGE 10

By the lakeside he sits staring, the water
a gentle, generous tongue lapping.
What if he'd been his mother's daughter
instead of her son? The wet clapping
of boats against the early morning docks
keeps time truer than household clocks
bonging hours from a distance
he can't understand. He has this one chance
at childhood, these ten years without end,
doors receding in lengthening halls
as he tries to approach. Won't he miss the fears
that come without reason, and friends,
and forgiveness, and the call he hears
rushing in answer whenever he calls?

LATE FIREWORKS

I want quiet, but it's the seventh
of July, the night the next town over

scheduled its explosions, mere
boomings here, echoes of flashes,

the inner thrumming of anxiety
itself. The neighbor's dog

squeals in anguish. My sleeping son
tosses, his dreamy panic punctuated

by sudden startled breaths. Now,
at last, comes the finale; if I stand

beside my garage, I can see the stars
fall between roofs. "That's the best

I've ever seen," I hear someone say
from a nearby lawn. Distant children

scream and clap and cheer, and
I resent their cataclysms.

Hiding inside bushes, I was a child
wild for privacy, safe

in the ring of my mother's eyes.
Now, I never forget myself, my son,

or anyone. I don't want more
reminders. I once ached to have been

born some long lost time ago, before
any noise, but I've grown and given

that wish away. Music drifts
from someone's yard, mumbles,

a party lingering in the wind. I wish
for nothing, for the world to simmer

to a soft hiss, a long life upon a dark
sea of grass rocking me to sleep.

SCRAP

The first draft of another night—
I'm nearly ready to scrap it for sleep.
I was taught, always, to do right
by a mother who raised me from deep
in the earth. She's been dead
twenty-three years—why do I feel the need
to write that again? I've said
it a thousand ways already, a creed
to me like a river's is water.
I'm out of ideas, but who needs them? At thirty-seven,
the only rhyme I can conjure is "daughter."
I don't believe in—while awaiting—heaven.
More my father now than I ever was his son,
I might have been, if not for myself, anyone.

CHECKED OFF

I thoroughly cleaned the basement this morning
and bought my daughter roller skates.
I complimented my wife on the necklace adorning
her neck and hand-washed the cheese-encrusted plates.

I treated my wart. I confirmed the time with my friend.
I filled the car with gas and did some exercise.
I listened to my favorite musician and let the music rend
my heart in two. I gave myself time to despise

our stupid, evil president. I read two poems.
I longed for immortality, for fame,
felt jealous of my fellow poets, my peers, my clones
who want exactly what I want, whose very names

boil my blood. I changed my son's dirty diaper
and replaced the new car's broken windshield wiper.

LONGEVITY

If only not wanting to die was enough to keep me alive.
If only that and the fear of death were the same,
or time was an ongoing negotiation, a kind of a game
one could play and maybe even win—*duck the scythe.*
If only terror was as mild and manageable as fear.
But terror is threaded with guilt, the *I did it* of dying,
all I put myself through, mistake after mistake, year after year,
that will leave no option, no desire after it all but lying
down for a good long rest. If only doing everything right—
eat vegetables, call my father, learn piano, exercise, play
with my kids—could indefinitely postpone the night.
If only I can tiptoe past disease and accident for another day,
to wake, to try, to hope, to believe in life, despite
the fact that *if only* won't forestall tomorrow, or make it stay.

10 ROCK HILL LANE

The car idling, kids and wife impatient but appeasing,
I stood out front snapping pictures with my phone.
Some later owner built a new house on the bones
of my old one, like a child given up at birth,
unaware of how the vanished parent shaped it.
I settled my family in a town just like that one,
only forty miles away, but in another state,
far enough to pretend I'd forgotten my template.
It's the same solution to the same problem:
how to raise a new family free of the chaos
of one's own youth, which one fled in search
of a new family, of one's own choosing, one's own
mistakes. Encoded, mustn't the past recreate itself?
Who, if not me, is my father? Where else am I but home?

HOW NOW

He walks along the shore with his daughter.
He's still young. They watch the water.
It's beautiful, though the waves are rough.
Being near it today, together, is enough.
This is a holy moment, he thinks hopefully,
the kind that will become a memory
to feed the thin heart on a dry day
when his daughter has grown and gone away.
But she's still right here, holding his hand
as waves roll in. She is—or was. He can't understand
what happened—they had only just
turned to go home, but more time must
have passed. A moment, and it's already now.
Where did she go? And when? And how?

BRIGHT BUSH

Instead of the same old turn
toward trusty disappointment,
my repository of well-worn
insight (e.g., *my days are ever intent*
on death and grief), a flowering:
this bush in our new front yard
explodes in sudden pink, showering
the air around with color. It's hard
not to be happy and hopeful about this—
life is bountiful, really about
how nature everywhere ravishes.
There is nothing here to doubt.
These petals will soon be brown and curled,
but they don't represent the whole world.

NEW JERSEY

I was afraid the past would catch up with me,
would find this new house too like the scarred
old childhood home. But it hasn't yet. A tree
casts soft and gentle shade over our green yard.
I feel forgiven all the sins I didn't commit
for long minutes at a time. What were they?
I can't now think of anything wrong with me—I fit
in these rooms, can mostly agree to each day.
For long minutes I don't even blame my mother
for dying, my father for spending years in bed.
My little traumas are just souvenirs of other
lives, of places I might have once visited.
I'm mostly a father here, a husband, barely a son.
The big sun rises early here, as I do, with everyone.

((5))

Thanks for Stopping By

ASSURANCES 4

There is always more work to do. A poem is never finished, only abandoned. A watched pot never boils. Watching a pot is excruciatingly boring.

~

One night is longer than three days.

~

My train is delayed. Does this mean I have more or less time?

~

Fate is applied in retrospect, like varnish, to protect the past from wear.

~

But I *want* to take my things with me.

~

Younger than me, they can't understand what I understand. Older than me, they can't understand what I understand.

~

In many ways my life is very rich. I go to concerts. I write poetry. I travel to Europe. I listen to my daughter as she unspools her strange and utterly startling thoughts. But in other ways, my life is very limited. *I* go to concerts. *I* write poetry. *I* travel to Europe. *I* listen to my daughter as she unspools her strange and utterly startling thoughts. I experience only what this *I* experiences. He has never tried ballet. He has never ridden a motorcycle. He has never been truly afraid for his life. He has never been hated. He can imagine all of these things, but only from *my* limited perspective. Sometimes he feels like his whole life is just a narrow hallway full of doors he doesn't open, though, he thinks, he may come back to them someday, open them then. But *someday* was yesterday, he thinks. He can't stop now. He has such a long way to go, and so little time, or time stretching in all directions. Which way? What door?

Because death happens to everyone else, we assume, it will happen to us. But haven't we been exceptions so far?

DEATH

Kids already asleep, the grown-ups sit out on the deck,
a few empty cans, an open bottle of wine on the table, I'm sure,

and stacked paper plates with half-eaten buns and dirty napkins.
From my backyard next door, I can hear them, the living, chatting.

I can't make out many words, mostly the rhythm, and laughing.
Death is not what they're discussing. "Goodnight,"

a woman says. "Goodnight," a few of them answer. A car
wakes, then its growl fades into the distance.

~

Wind rises and falls, telling
the trees to tell one another.
Air conditioners hum forever.

~

Clocks ticking. Grains of falling sand.
What else is there to think about?

But what is the thought? Some small animal
crunching around in the ivy. A plane

arching across or falling from the sky.
Endless seas stretching toward the horizon.

And beyond the horizon? Friends?
Memories? Quiet and perfect calm?

A small boat? A loving hospital?
An air conditioner humming me to sleep?

It came as a surprise to me:
that mothers die, that mine did
so young, when I was so young, when she
was younger than my wife is now.

It still seems so unlikely, after
waking another morning in my bed,
not to wake, the least likely
and least lifelike thing.

She won't answer
the phone, mail a present, or ever
have met her grandchildren.
And she'll never die again.

Moths crowd and lunge at
the light above my driveway,
making a flicking sound
as they hit the bulb, the siding.

How quietly the shock begins,
like thunder rolling in,
                    so softly at first
one mistakes it for something else,

each generation learning alone,
anew, each of us privately aghast,

embarrassed, hiding as if until
it passes,
            this one, long night.

A man riding a bike in New York was hit by a car and killed
last week, if a newspaper story
about the fourteen biking deaths this year
is to be believed. It's an emergency,
the mayor declared.
This is merely what happens. And so,
and yet, each morning I bike south
from the Port Authority to my office.

~

Within three years, Totoro, our family hamster, will die.
Hamsters simply don't live longer. Scientists theorize
that there are tortoises alive today that are over five hundred
years old, and a clam has been found that, according to scientists,
was born in 1499, before Shakespeare.
Imagine the moment that clam began its incomparable epoch.
Montezuma and Napoleon and Emily Dickinson
passed through its years. Churchill and Hitler,
Kennedy and Martin Luther King Jr., Frank Zappa,
and my Aunt Fabienne lived and died. Leonardo and Pollack
were that clam's contemporaries. The Troubles,
Woodstock, Tiananmen Square, "We Didn't Start the Fire." Shortly
after I graduated from college, that clam was accidentally killed.

~

My whole life
is a blip
to a tortoise,

a single unthundering
tick of God's
imaginary watch.

I want to do something
my friends and my children
and their children's
children might remember,
to die famous for succeeding
at the things I love best,

writing poetry and
talking late into the night
about music and teaching
and supporting the careers
of younger writers and caring
for my disabled son and learning
year by year to be kinder
and less defensive.

I like to imagine myself, too,
in an ashen near-future, huddled in
a shack cobbled of refuse harvested
from the rubble, helping
others escape through
a network of secret tunnels,
a rare green leaf pressed
between the pages
of the last beloved book.

Words
like mine live
and die
in lives like mine.

The clam was born in 1499.
Dorothea was born in 1910.
My grandmother was born in 1912.
Richard was born in 1926.
My dad was born in 1946.
My mom was born in 1947.
Bill Callahan was born in 1966.
Brenda was born in 1970.
I was born in 1979.
Cal was born in 2007.
Simone was born in 2011.
Totoro was born in 2019.
Cashew, the puppy, was born in 2020

~

Crickets chirping everywhere,
the ambient din of still air.
I *might* have wasted my life.

~

And what about my *things*—
books, CDs, records, hats, guitars, devices,
souvenirs, these weights placed
along the edges of my life

to keep the wind from lifting it away.
I treasure them not because
they are precious or rare,
but because they are *mine*—

I gathered them and put them in order
according to the alphabet
of my affections, my obsessions'
persistent foreword counting,

stacked them like bricks against
storms past, passing, and to come.
I hold them with the mortar of my wishes
and greed. Will they degrade

to mere things again, disbursed
to distant eBay buyers, landfills,
and future generations unable to decipher
the soul-map of which they're scraps?

~

I search for Totoro, peering
into the various hideouts in his cage.
He is present everywhere
in our home, a small ambassador

from a country on this side
of the horizon, a sure sign,
a whole soul in a body
the size and color of a Twinkie.

He pulls me toward him,
a pinprick in the hull of the plane,
which is not falling from the sky
but moving through it

in the only direction it can,
the only one there is, slicing
through hope and dread,
which are thin and invisible

as air, which drags and pulls
at the plane overhead,
slowing it down
as it holds it up.

The sun rises each day like a fathomless eye.
The earth choruses randomly at every instant.

I wish my wife and daughter were home
from their trip. No one can ever come

close enough. The party next door is dying
down, just three or four friends left, still laughing,

a playlist of 1990s top 40 hits
rippling through the infinite suburban night.

ASSURANCES 5

Fear is always happy to compromise.

~

We don't know what we don't know, of course, and so can be forgiven. But how much of what we know do we know? Who measures that and says how much to forgive?

~

Alcohol: blunt-edged tool for digging up more childhood. Works poorly, but relatively cheap.

~

No proof and so much to prove.

~

He wrote 300 songs, he claims. More likely, he wrote three songs 100 times each.

~

Hatred: anger at the self pointed backwards.

~

Suicide: anger at others pointed backwards.

~

How I know I'm not young anymore: I no longer dismiss this thought.

It takes only a week or two to feel at home anywhere—*anywhere*.

Anything big and heavy is a key.

I will almost certainly die without learning to speak French, no matter how long it takes.

The bottom: no one can dig forever.

ACKNOWLEDGMENTS

Thank you to the editors of the following publications, in which some of these poems appeared, sometimes in slightly different versions:

Ambit (UK): "Late Fireworks;
American Poetry Review: "Death";
The Awl: "Worry";
Colorado Review: "Marriage Abstract" ("Arguments . . ."), "How Now" "Assurances 2";
Conduit: "A Dream I Never Had," "I Am A Father Now";
Copper Nickel: "Dread on the Eve of My Daughter's Seventh Birthday Party";
Four Way Review: "Regret," "What You Love," "Disappointment";
Gulf Coast: "Gush," "The True Work";
Kenyon Review Online: "Tying a Garbage Bag," "Marriage Abstract (Finally . . .)";
The Nation: "Folded Note";
The Paris Review: "List";
Poem A Day: "Lifted," "Immortality," "New Jersey";
Poetry International: "Distillation," "Early to Bed";
The New Yorker: "Peers," "Son," "The Chorus";
Tin House: "Fable of the Man by the Water."

Parts of section 3 originally appeared as the chapbook *Ambivalence and Other Conundrums* (Omnidawn Publishing in 2014). Thank you to Rusty and Ken for commissioning these poems and working with me on them.

"I Am a Father Now" also appeared in *The Best American Poetry 2020*, edited by Paisley Rekdal and David Lehman.

Thank you, New Jersey, especially as personified by Wendy Gould-Nogueira, Chris Hardy, Kate Hardy, Addie Kauffman, Ross Kaufman, and Gin Russo. And thank you to many friends, in alphabetical order, who have supported the writing of this book:

Sonya Balchandani, Jesse Ball, Mark Bibbins, Jenny Boully, Jericho Brown, Stephanie Burt, Brian Chambers, Penny Cray, Laura Cronk, John DeLore, Michael Dumanis, Eliza Factor, Gibson Fay-LeBlanc, Danny Felsenfeld, Kelly Forsythe, Gabe Fried, Woody Fu, Forrest Gander, Elizabeth Gold, Rachel Eliza Griffiths, Helena de Groot, Cathy Park Hong, Richard Howard, Dorothea Lasky, Dana Levin, Sebastian Marx, Wayne Miller, Michael Morse, Meghan O'Rourke, Derek Palacio, the *Paris Review* crew, Jason Pendrock, Maya C. Popa, D. A. Powell, Minna Proctor, Kevin Prufer, Didi Rybak, Carey Salerno, Robyn Schiff, Nicole Sealey, Jonny Segura, Natalie Shapero, Jeff Shotts, Carmen Giménez Smith, Darin Strauss, Mary Szybist, Nick Twemlow, Jillian Weise, Mark Wunderlich, Monica Youn, and Rachel Zucker.

Thank you to Chris Bennem and Lisa Moore of Glen Hollow, where some of these poems were revised.

"Gush" borrows a line from T. S. Eliot's "The Love Song of J. Alfred Prufrock."

Thank you to Peter Conners and everyone at BOA Editions, Ltd. for more than a decade of support and enthusiasm for my work—I feel very lucky.

Thank you to my children, Cal and Simone, who are the horizon toward which this adventure is bound.

ABOUT THE AUTHOR

Craig Morgan Teicher is the author of three previous poetry collections, most recently *The Trembling Answers*, which won the 2017 Lenore Marshall Poetry Prize from the Academy of American Poets. He is also the author of the essay collection *We Begin in Gladness: How Poets Progress* and *Cradle Book: Stories and Fables*. He teaches creative writing at NYU and Bennington College, works at *The Paris Review*, and lives in New Jersey with his wife, children, dog, and hamster.

BOA EDITIONS, LTD.
AMERICAN POETS CONTINUUM SERIES

COLOPHON

BOA Editions, Ltd., a not-for-profit publisher of poetry and other literary works, fosters readership and appreciation of contemporary literature. By identifying, cultivating, and publishing both new and established poets and selecting authors of unique literary talent, BOA brings high-quality literature to the public.

Support for this effort comes from the sale of its publications, grant funding, and private donations.

◎ ◎ ◎

The publication of this book is made possible, in part, by the special support of the following individuals:

Anonymous (x2)
Anya Backlund, Blue Flower Arts
June C. Baker
Susan Burke & Bill Leonardi, *in honor of Boo Poulin*
The Chris Dahl & Ruth Rowse Charitable Fund
Susan DeWitt Davie
Margaret Heminway
Grant Holcomb
Kathleen C. Holcombe
Nora A. Jones
Paul LaFerriere & Dorrie Parini
Jack & Gail Langerak
Melanie & Ron Martin-Dent
Joe McElveney
Stephen & Theo Munson
Boo Poulin
Deborah Ronnen
Elizabeth Spenst
William Waddel & Linda Rubel
Michael Waters & Mihaela Moscaliuc